THE UNOFFICIAL GUIDE TO

MrBeast AND BEYOND

AWESOME FACTS INSPIRED BY THE YOUTUBE SENSATION

BY PATTY MICHAELS • ILLUSTRATED BY CEEJ ROWLAND

Simon Spotlight
New York Amsterdam/Antwerp London
Toronto Sydney/Melbourne New Delhi

For my daughter, Cassidy Grace
—P. M.

To Gosia, the kids,
and Mum and Dad
—C. R.

SIMON SPOTLIGHT
An imprint of Simon & Schuster Children's Publishing Division
1230 Avenue of the Americas, New York, New York 10020

This Simon Spotlight edition December 2025

at 1-866-248-3049 or visit our website at www.simonspeakers.com.
This book is not authorized, endorsed, or sponsored by any person or entity owning or controlling any rights in the MrBeast name, products, or trademarks.
For information about special discounts for bulk purchases, please contact Simon & Schuster Special Sales at 1-866-506-1949 or business@simonandschuster.com.
Simon & Schuster strongly believes in freedom of expression and stands against censorship in all its forms.
For more information, visit BooksBelong.com.
The Simon & Schuster Speakers Bureau can bring authors to your live event.
For more information or to book an event, contact the Simon & Schuster Speakers Bureau
Text by Patty Michaels
Book design by Laura Roode
Interior photos: p. 6: iStock/Ponchikz (top), iStock/scaliger (bottom); p. 10: iStock/Olekcii Mech (first-aid kit), iStock/Jean-philippe WALLET (beach); p. 11: iStock/Olav Thokle; p. 13: iStock/RobertMayne; p. 14: iStock/InnerPeaceSeeker (top), iStock/ImageCraft Co (bottom; also on p. 18); p. 16: iStock/PeterHermesFurian (map vignette), iStock/Anton Aleksenko (main); p. 17: iStock/pius99; p. 18: iStock/S_Bachstroem (bottom); p. 21: iStock/PeterHermesFurian (map), iStock/anyaberkut (main); p. 22: iStock/Roman Chekhovskoy (top), iStock/Diy13 (bottom); p. 24: iStock/Believe_In_Me; p. 25: iStock/sportpoint (top), iStock/Stockyme (middle), iStock/Elena Zolotova (bottom); p. 27: iStock/mrjo2405 (snake, top), iStock/wing-wing (sky, top), iStock/Ali Çobanoğlu (bottom left), iStock/reptiles4all (bottom right); p. 29: iStock/GettyTim82 (left), iStock/alex-mit (right); p. 30: iStock/gustavomellossa; p. 32: iStock/Hashbu Production; p. 33: iStock/laurence soulez; p. 34: iStock/jotily; p. 35: iStock/Pla2na; p. 36: iStock/Flavio Treppner; p. 35: iStock/fotogal (bottom); p. 37: iStock/Nevena1987 (top left), iStock/Eudyptula (top right), iStock/oatawa (bottom)
The text of this book was set in Redonda.
Manufactured in the United States of America 1025 LAK
2 4 6 8 10 9 7 5 3 1
Library of Congress Cataloging-in-Publication Data
Names: Michaels, Patty author | Rowland, Ceej illustrator
Title: MrBeast and beyond! : wacky facts inspired by the You Tube sensation / by Patty Michaels ; illustrated by Ceej Rowland.
Description: Simon Spotlight hardcover edition. | New York : Simon Spotlight, 2025. | Summary: "A fully illustrated book of fun facts inspired by the sensational YouTube channel MrBeast, chock-full of weird facts and funky figures about the locations and challenges featured in his top-viewed videos"—Provided by publisher. Identifiers: LCCN 2025020797 | ISBN 9798347104192 hardback | ISBN 9798347104208 ebook
Subjects: LCSH: MrBeast, 1998– —Juvenile literature | YouTube (Firm)—Juvenile literature | Internet personalities—Biography—Juvenile literature
Classification: LCC PN1992.9236.M73 M53 2025
LC record available at https://lccn.loc.gov/2025020797

CHAPTER 1
Meet MrBeast!

***MrBeast** is one of the most popular social media personalities in the world, and his YouTube channel has hundreds of millions of subscribers! But how much do you really know about this popular influencer? (After all, having a real name like MrBeast would be pretty silly!)*

MrBeast's real name is **JAMES STEPHEN DONALDSON**, and his nickname is Jimmy. He was born on May 7, 1998, in Wichita, Kansas, but grew up in North Carolina. Jimmy started his YouTube channel when he was 13 years old. At first he would post videos of himself playing video games, but then he began creating and posting videos where he would perform stunts. His online following skyrocketed, and the rest, well, it's pretty much MrBeast history!

Since then MrBeast has posted videos, stunts, and contests with some of his childhood friends known as "the Beast Gang." As his videos became more successful, MrBeast grew his business to include food delivery services, chocolate bar production, and reality TV. MrBeast's many income streams have helped to make him one of the richest and most successful YouTubers in the world!

CHAPTER 2
Scary Survival
HELP

The Beast Gang has performed some super scary stunts. From (gulp!) being buried alive to stranding themselves on a desert island, they have raised the fear factor! Could you survive these challenges?

Buried Alive!

MrBeast survived for seven days in a coffin under thousands of pounds of dirt—some people's worst nightmare! Is it one of yours?

DID YOU KNOW? In the 17th century, sick people may have occasionally been buried because they were thought to be dead, but they were still alive! In order for people not to be mistakenly buried alive, safety coffins were later designed with a bell they could ring to be rescued.

SAVED BY THE BELL!

George Washington, America's first president, feared being buried alive. He gave specific instructions not to bury him for at least three days after he died in case he was still alive. When he did pass away, a doctor named William Thornton hoped maybe he could bring him back to life. But unfortunately, that was not possible. The president's remains were buried in his family tomb at his home, Mount Vernon, alongside other family members.

A tragic tale of a woman being buried alive not once but TWICE occurred in Basingstoke, England, in 1674. The first time she was rescued, she had been so severely injured after trying to escape from the coffin that she showed no sign of life—so she was put back in her coffin. It turned out she was still alive, and when they opened the coffin again, it appeared that she had once more tried to claw her way out!

Poet Edgar Allan Poe wrote a short story in 1844 called "The Premature Burial." In the story the narrator suffers from catalepsy (a state where your limbs are frozen in place) and is buried alive. How scary is that?!

Stranded!

MrBeast stayed on a desert island, where civilization had not lived for over 250 years, for seven whole days! Would you be up to the challenge?

If you think you could live on a desert island, you'll definitely need to follow these **SURVIVAL TIPS**:

- Always travel with a first aid kit.
- Learn how to perform CPR.
- Know how to swim—water safety is essential!
- Build a shelter using natural materials like wood, grass, and sticks.

Living on a remote island may not be your thing, but a lot of animals call those places home. Near the Indian Ocean, the Kerguelen Islands are home to mammals like seals and penguins. And a snowy, icy island named Spitsbergen in Norway has a large population of polar bears!

The Abandoned City Challenge

MrBeast and the gang spent seven days and nights in an abandoned city! They had to find a safe space to build shelter so they could sleep and stay warm. Sounds pretty spooky!

Even though completely abandoned places are rare, they do exist! An island called la Isla de las Muñecas in Mexico is one of the scariest abandoned places ever. Rumor has it in the 1950s the island's caretaker found a doll near the spot where a young girl was thought to have drowned years earlier. He hung the doll from a tree in remembrance of her, and he claimed to discover new dolls strung up from trees every time he went outside. The girl supposedly haunted him from beyond the grave for the rest of his days. The island is now abandoned—except for hundreds of those creepy dolls.

A town called Bodie, located in a desert in California, was founded in the late 1800s. After a ruinous fire in 1932 and the end of mining in 1942, Bodie slipped into abandonment. It was named a National Historic Site around 1962.

In South Korea the amusement park Okpo Land stood abandoned for years, with all its structures still in place. As if roller coasters weren't scary enough!

CHAPTER 3
Around the World

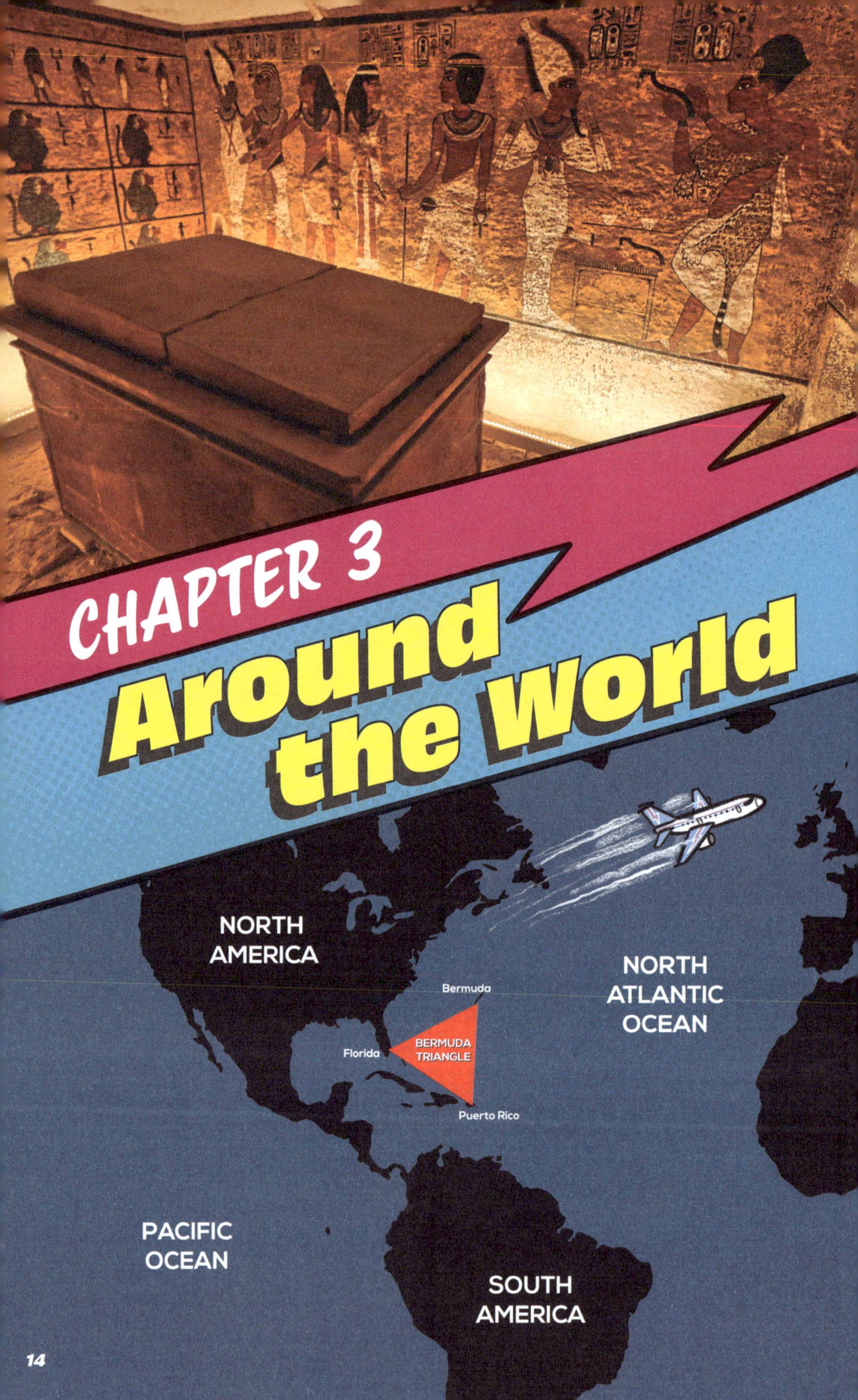

Wouldn't it be awesome to travel with your besties? MrBeast and his friends have been to some pretty cool places—but some of these places are rumored to be pretty dangerous, too. (A chill beach vacation or a fun trip to an amusement park, they are not!)

Pyramids of Giza

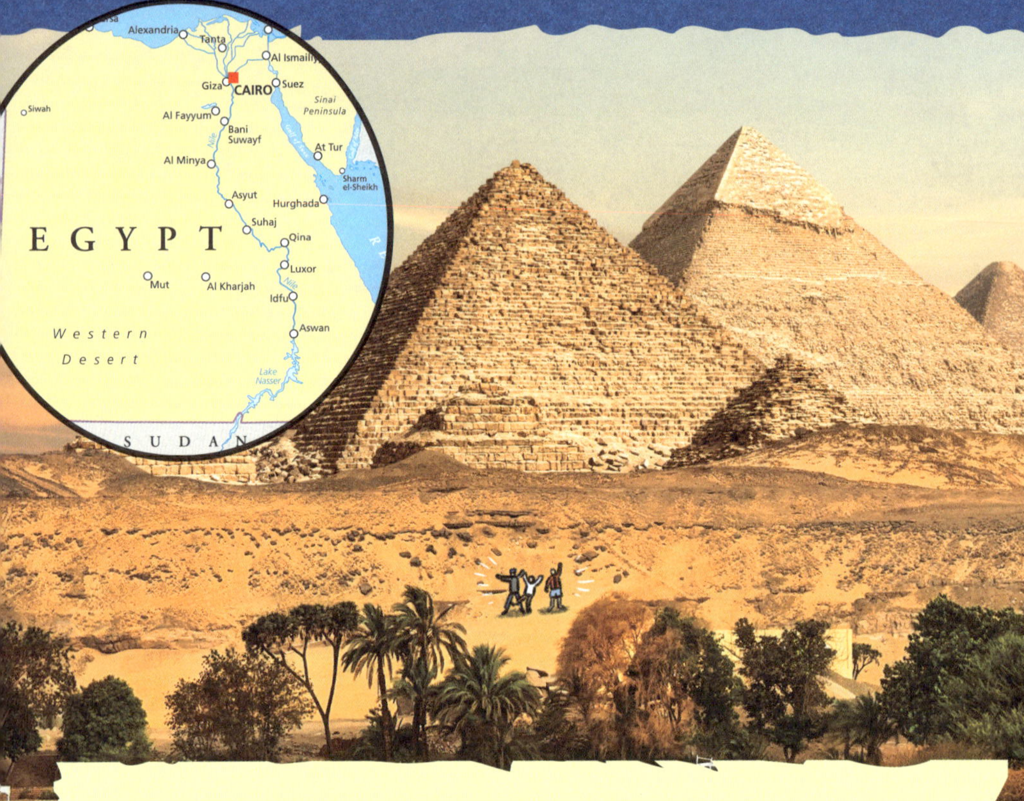

Jimmy and his friends had the pyramids all to themselves for 100 hours—how cool is that?!—and learned all about these amazing ancient structures!

The Pyramids of Giza are considered one of the Seven Wonders of the Ancient World. They are located in Egypt near the Nile River and were built as royal tombs for three different pharaohs. To this day, scientists are unsure exactly how the pyramids were built but believe that a system of ramps, ropes, and levers combined to create a true feat of ancient engineering!

One of the most amazing creations near these pyramids is the Great Sphinx. It has a face resembling a person's and a body resembling a lion's, and it was carved from a single enormous piece of limestone!

Inside the pyramids are a ton of ancient passageways and—in some spots—not a lot of oxygen. Jimmy and his friends even swam through a secret underground tomb buried wayyyy underneath the pyramids. A historic adventure!

Bermuda Triangle

MrBeast and the Beast Gang spent 24 hours in this infamous spot in the ocean! Luckily, they made it back home safely—but not everyone, or everything, does . . .

Bermuda
Florida
BERMUDA TRIANGLE
Puerto Rico

The Bermuda Triangle (also known as the "Devil's Triangle") has been called one of THE most dangerous places in the world. It's a patch of ocean in the shape of a triangle, with its three points at the Florida coast, Bermuda, and Puerto Rico (part of the Greater Antilles islands).

More than 50 ships and 20 planes have mysteriously disappeared there and left no trace. There are many conspiracy theories surrounding the disappearances. Some people think aliens or supernatural events may be at work! However, a scientist from Australia named Karl Kruszelnicki believes that a combination of severe weather, simple human mistakes, and heavy air and sea traffic is to blame, a theory supported today by the United States Coast Guard and the National Oceanic and Atmospheric Administration (NOAA).

Amazing Antarctica

MrBeast and his gang braved the freezing temperatures of Antarctica for 50 hours! Could you survive like they did?

Antarctica is one of the most fascinating and mysterious places in the world. Not only is it cold and icy, with an average temperature of zero degrees Fahrenheit, but it's also one of the driest places in the world as well, with only two inches of rainfall per year!

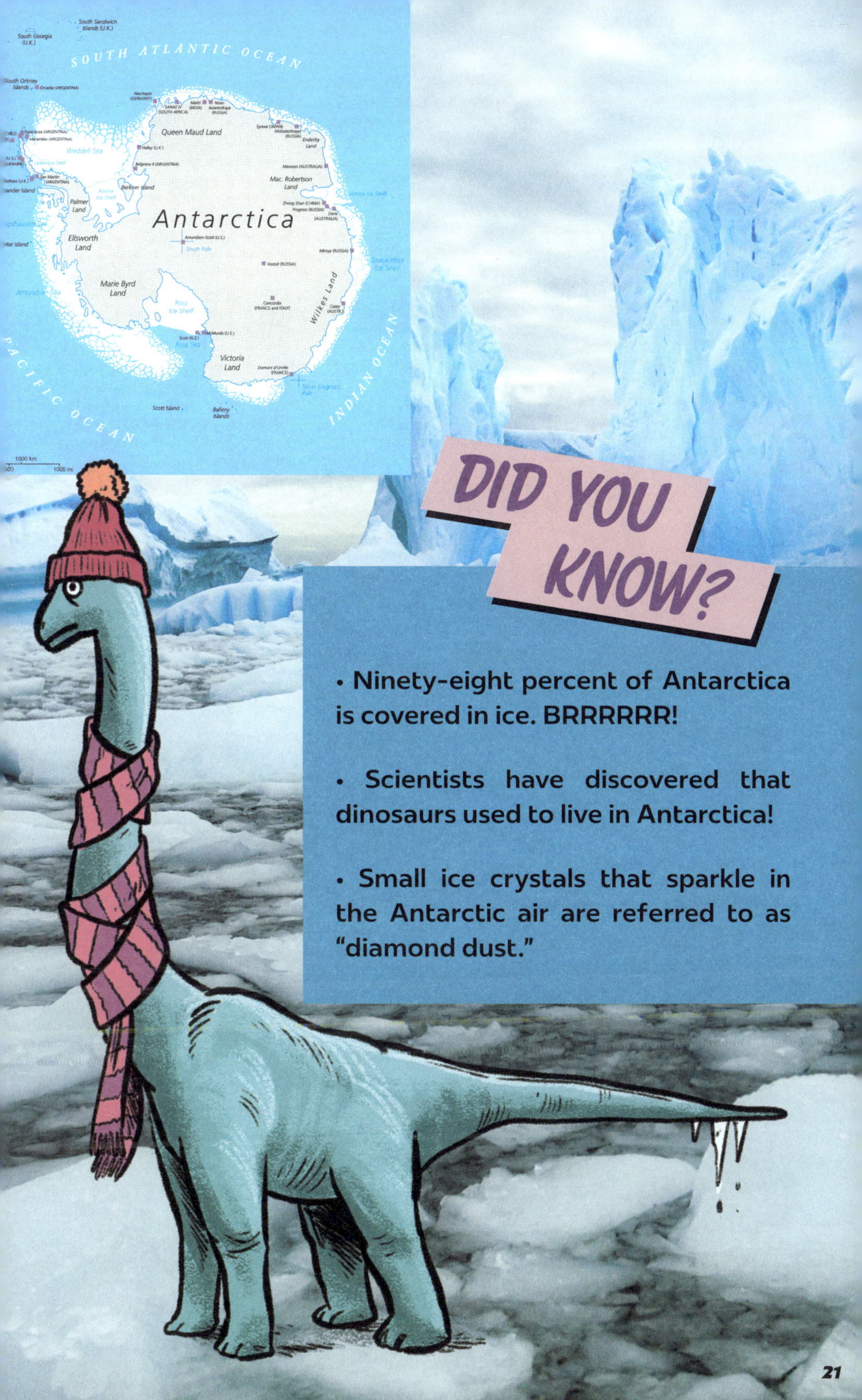

DID YOU KNOW?

- Ninety-eight percent of Antarctica is covered in ice. BRRRRRR!
- Scientists have discovered that dinosaurs used to live in Antarctica!
- Small ice crystals that sparkle in the Antarctic air are referred to as "diamond dust."

CHAPTER 4
Crazy Challenges

ABSOLUTELY WILD!
3812...
MrBeast and his crew have participated in some pretty intense stunts, but these challenges prove that FEAR is not a word that exists in MrBeast's vocabulary!
BANANAS!
NO WAY!

Ferris Wheel Frenzy

MrBeast and the crew rode a thousand laps around a Ferris wheel—through cold, dizziness, darkening skies, and, well, just plain boredom! Would you give this challenge a spin?

If you've been to a carnival or amusement park, you've probably seen a Ferris wheel, but they weren't always so common. Engineer George Washington Gale Ferris Jr. pitched the idea of the very first Ferris wheel in 1892, as a major attraction for the upcoming Columbian Exposition fair in Chicago. He was laughed out of the room and called the "Man with Wheels in His Head"! Ferris had to fight for his wheel to be built, but it paid off: More than one million people rode it over the four-month fair, and now Ferris wheels are widely known.

WHEELS AROUND THE WORLD!

• The tallest Ferris wheel in the world is the **AIN DUBAI**, located on an island off Dubai in the United Arab Emirates—it's 820 feet high!

• The **SINGAPORE FLYER** offers four-course meals in its cabins and is 541 feet tall. That's roughly the same height as 31 giraffes!

• The **LONDON EYE** is one of the world's most famous Ferris wheels, with panoramic views of London's landmarks. It's also known as the Millennium Wheel, since it opened in the year 2000.

Slithering Snakes

MrBeast challenged his crew to sit in a bathtub full of snakes for a $10,000 prize! Would you put yourself in this slippery situation?

Even though snakes can be intimidating, they are special creatures—and they aren't actually slimy! Snakes are covered in dry, scaly skin that they shed every few months, and bird feathers and mammal hair are thought to have evolved from those very scales.

DID YOU KNOW?

- Snakes use their tongues to smell.
- Snake venom can be deadly, but it can also be used to create medicine.
- Snakes do not have ears, but they can hear through their jaws.
- Some snakes can glide through the air, making it appear that they can fly!

Make It Count!

You've probably heard of counting sheep to fall asleep. But can you imagine counting to 10,000, or 100,000, or even 200,000, like MrBeast did in his challenges? Now that's a LOT of sheep.

Doesn't that make you tired just thinking about it?!

COUNT 'EM—HERE ARE FOUR FUN FACTS ABOUT NUMBERS!

- A study from 2015 counted more than **THREE TRILLION** trees on Earth!
- The Milky Way consists of at least **ONE HUNDRED BILLION** stars!
- The number of grains of sand on the planet is nearly impossible to measure but might total as high as an **OCTILLION**!
- The universe is **13.8 BILLION** years old!

ALL THOSE -ILLION NUMBERS SEEM PRETTY BIG . . . BUT HOW BIG ARE THEY, ACTUALLY?

- A million $1 bills laid end to end would stretch about 95 miles, roughly the distance from New York to Philadelphia—but a billion $1 bills end to end would reach about 96,900 miles, enough to wrap around the Earth nearly four times!

- If you counted one number every second, to count to a million would take about 11 days. To count to a billion, it would take about 31 years. And to count to a trillion would take 31,709 years!

- A *googol* is the number one followed by one hundred zeros—and a googolplex is a one followed by a googol of zeros!

10,000,000,000,000,000,000,000,000,000,000,000,000,000,000,000,000,000,000,000,000,000,000,000,000,000,000,000,000,000,000,000,000,000,000,000,000

CHAPTER 5
Giving Back

An important part of MrBeast's mission is to do helpful things for good causes. Giving back makes the world go 'round!

Beach Cleaning

Beaches and oceans around the world have become littered with trash. Luckily, MrBeast helped to clear tons of trash from local beaches.

Every single day 13,000 to 15,000 pieces of plastic are thrown in the ocean—and the garbage builds up because a lot of the trash that is disposed of improperly is not biodegradable.

THE GREAT PACIFIC GARBAGE PATCH, also known as the Pacific trash vortex, is an area of the ocean named for how full of litter it is! It's about 620,000 square miles, nearly twice the size of Texas.

More than 100,000 marine animals are found dead every year from ingesting or getting stuck in plastic in the ocean—and that's only counting the ones that are found, not the ones that likely sink to the ocean floor. Not to mention that roughly a million sea birds die from plastic annually. It's our responsibility to dispose of waste so that we don't harm our natural environment!

Tree Planting

MrBeast and his crew helped plant 20 MILLION trees as one of their challenges. What can you do to contribute to our planet?

Trees are a vital natural resource. They provide habitats, food, and oxygen and help to support wildlife. How much do you know about trees? Check out these facts to learn more!

• Most tree roots are located in only the top 6 to 24 inches of soil.
• A tree with lots of leaves can absorb up to 150 gallons of water a DAY! That is one thirsty tree!
• Some of the largest pinecones in the world can be found in trees located in southern California. These pinecones can weigh up to 10 pounds!

Dog Rescuing

In 2023 MrBeast rescued 100 dogs from an animal shelter and brought them to an animal sanctuary, where they were put up for adoption—and all 100 dogs found wonderful homes!

Dogs are one of the most beloved pets in America—but they originally evolved from wolves! Over time, their teeth, paws, and skulls got smaller, making them easier for humans to domesticate (to keep as pets). Some dogs are considered to be as smart as a two-year-old human and can learn over 100 words!

DID YOU KNOW?

- Dogs can only sweat from their paws and nose. In hot weather, dogs stay cool by panting.

- Dogs, just like humans, can be right- or left-handed. (In their case, right- or left-pawed!)

- A dog's sense of smell is more than ten thousand times stronger than a human's!

- Dogs are good for your health—studies have shown that petting a dog for 15 minutes lowers blood pressure and helps you feel less lonely!

Test Your MrBeast Knowledge!

Now that you've finished reading this book, how well do you know everything about this famous YouTuber and the world of his videos? Take this quiz below and find out!

1. What number did MrBeast *not* count to in one of his videos?

   A. 10,000
   B. 350,000
   C. 100,000
   D. 200,000

2. What kind of candy does MrBeast produce?

   A. Saltwater taffy
   B. Jelly beans
   C. Chocolate bars
   D. Lollipops

3. How tall is the tallest Ferris wheel in the world?

   A. 820 feet
   B. 1500 feet
   C. 542 feet
   D. 675 feet

4. On what cold-weather continent did MrBeast and the Beast Gang camp outside for 50 hours?

A. Iceland
B. Antarctica
C. Sweden
D. Switzerland

5. How many dogs did MrBeast rescue and bring to an animal sanctuary?

A. 50
B. 75
C. 100
D. 25

6. What did MrBeast plant 20 million of?

A. Bushes
B. Trees
C. Tomato plants
D. Sunflowers

7. What is MrBeast's real name?

A. Chandler Geller
B. Nate Draper
C. Kyle Depp
D. James Stephen Donaldson

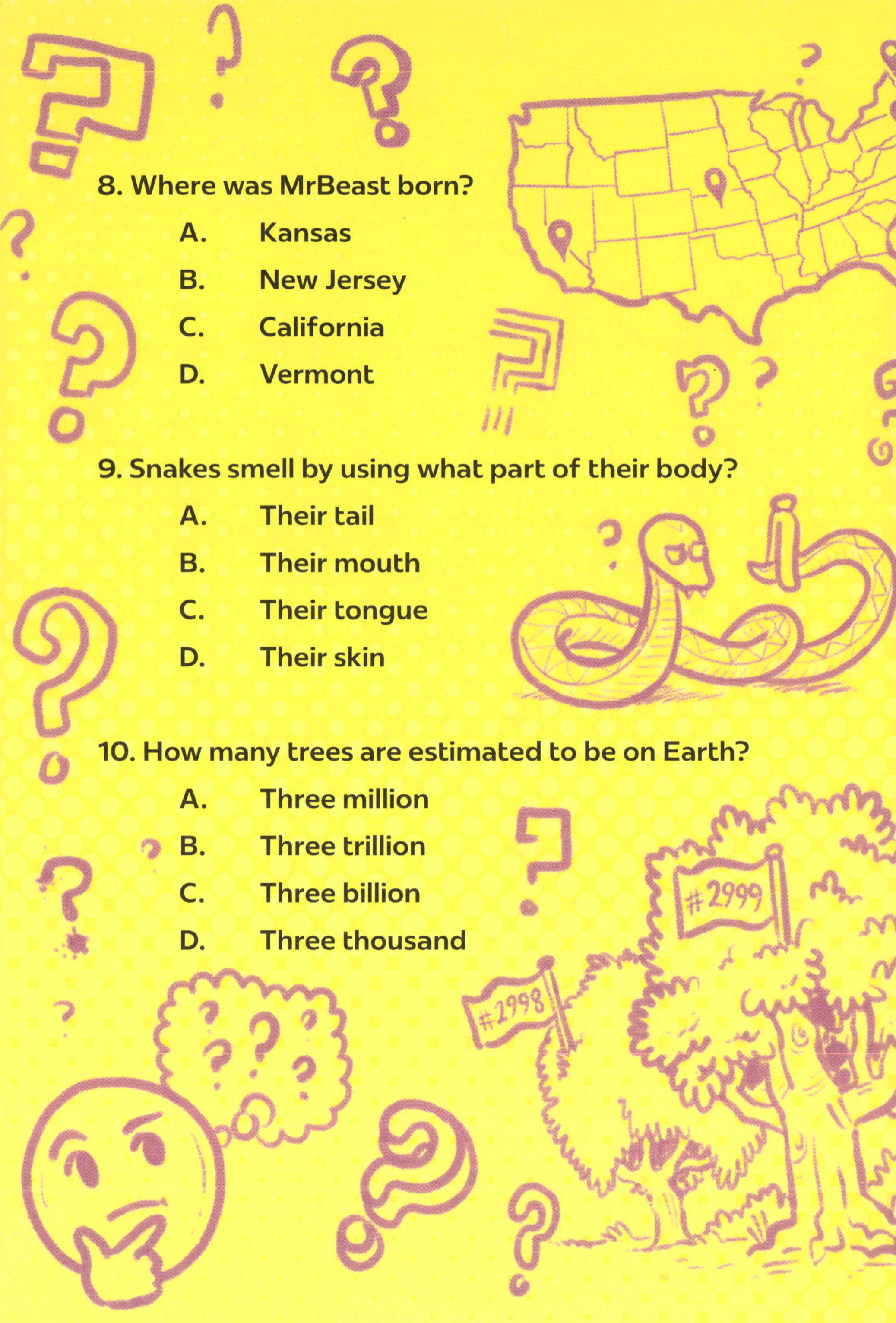

8. Where was MrBeast born?

- A. Kansas
- B. New Jersey
- C. California
- D. Vermont

9. Snakes smell by using what part of their body?

- A. Their tail
- B. Their mouth
- C. Their tongue
- D. Their skin

10. How many trees are estimated to be on Earth?

- A. Three million
- B. Three trillion
- C. Three billion
- D. Three thousand

ANSWERS: 1. B; 2. C; 3. A; 4. B; 5. C; 6. B; 7. D; 8. A; 9. C; 10. B